Speak Up

Book 1

Listening and Pronunciation for Beginning Students

Cheryl Pavlik

NEWBURY HOUSE

Heinle & Heinle Publishers

I(T)P An International Thomson Publishing Company

Pacific Grove • Albany • Bonn • Boston • Cincinnati • Detroit • London • Madrid • Melbourne
Mexico City • New York • Paris • San Francisco • Tokyo • Toronto • Washington

The Publication of *Speak Up—Book 1, Second Edition* was directed by the members of the Newbury House Publishing Team at Heinle & Heinle:

Erik Gundersen, *Editorial Director*
John F. McHugh, *Market Development Director*
Kristin Thalheimer, *Production Services Coordinator*
Elizabeth Holthaus, *Team Leader and Director of Production*

Also participating in the publication of this program were:

Publisher: Stanley J. Galek
Project Manager: Linda Lee
Assistant Editor: Karen P. Hazar
Associate Production Editor: Maryellen Eschmann
Manufacturing Coordinator: Mary Beth Hennebury
Photo Researcher: Philippe Heckly
Photo Specialist: Jonathan Stark
Interior Designer: Carol H. Rose
Illustrator: Bob Holmes
Cover Artist and Designer: Kim Wedlake

LIBRARY OF CONGRESS CATALOGING-IN PUBLICATION DATA

Pavlik, Cheryl, 1949-
    Speak up / Cheryl Pavlik
        p.   cm.
    Contents: bk. 1. Listening and pronunciation for beginning
students — bk. 2. Listening and pronunciation for high beginning
students.
    ISBN 0-8384-4996-4 (v. 1.). — ISBN 0-8384-4998-0 (v. 2.)
    1. English language — Textbooks for foreign speakers. 2. English
language — Pronunciation — Problems, exercises, etc.
3. Listening Pronunciation — Problems, exercises, etc. I. Title.
PE1128.P377 1995
428.3'4—dc20   94–25204
                                                           CIP

Heinle & Heinle Publishers/A Division of International Thomson Publishing, Inc.

Manufactured in the United States of America
ISBN 0-8384-4996-4

10 9 8 7 6 5 4 3 2 1

Table of Contents

To the Teacher   v

	Unit Title	Pronunciation Focus	Page

To the Teacher

Speak Up is a comprehensive two-level oral/aural skills program for beginning and high beginning students of English as a second or foreign language (ESL/EFL). Book 1 is designed for beginning level students, Book 2 for high beginners. *Speak Up* presents engaging and relevant contexts that provide students ample opportunity to develop their pronunciation, listening comprehension, and speaking skills.

Since *Speak Up Book 1* is designed for beginning ESL and EFL students, every effort has been made to control structures to those featured in beginning textbooks and courses. Vocabulary is also strictly controlled where comprehension is necessary. However, low-frequency words can sometimes be found in the pronunciation exercises, where practicing the production of specific sounds is the central goal.

Organization of the Text

Speak Up Book 1 is divided into three sections. Each section contains nine units and a review. The first two sections cover consonant contrasts and the last section deals with vowel contrasts. There are two exceptions to this division. Because of their importance, final *-er* and the vowel contrast in *can/can't* are presented in the first section.

New to the Second Edition

Speak Up Book 1 has been comprehensively revised. As the new titles of each unit suggest, every effort has been made to embed specific listening comprehension and pronunciation instruction in relevant and natural contexts. All of the content is either updated or new.

There are three new key features in the second edition. The first is **Before you begin**. This is meant as a short warm-up activity to get students thinking about the topic. The second new feature is a communicative exercise that is meant to give students a chance to practice the material in a less-structured way. The third new feature is the inclusion of mouth diagrams and a vowel chart in the back of the text.

Unit Organization

As in the first edition, Section A is a conversation that incorporates the target language presented within the unit. In this section, students are first directed to read the pre-listening comprehension questions. Section B follows with sound discrimination and pronunciation exercises. Sections C and D generally present and practice related material such as syllables, stress, intonation, and listening to reduced speech.

Using the Text

Before you begin. The purpose of this section is to promote student involvement in the situational context of the conversation. It can be done with the entire class, as groupwork or pairwork. Students working on their own in the laboratory should be encouraged to read the questions and think about the answers. This section should take no more than five minutes of class time.

Section A. It is important that students read the listening comprehension questions before they actually listen to the conversation. This will aid their comprehension by providing them with a focus. If students seem dubious after listening to the conversation once, do not hesitate to play it for them again before you go over the answers to the questions.

Sections B-D. These sections provide practice in sound discrimination, stress, intonation, and listening to reduced speech. In these sections students may encounter unknown and obscure vocabulary words that have been included for practice of particular sounds. Students should be encouraged to repeat the words even though they may not understand them.

Students may easily become frustrated trying to pronounce difficult sounds. Make sure they understand that being able to hear these difficult sounds is an important preliminary step to being able to pronounce them and that they should not feel discouraged if they cannot say them immediately.

Section E. Since this section usually contains freer activities, there are times that students will be able to avoid the target language if they want. Therefore, teachers should encourage their students to use the structures and sounds of the unit as much as possible. It may sometimes be helpful to precede the activity with a model that uses some of the target language.

Mouth Diagrams and Vowel Chart

Many students will be unfamiliar with the use of the mouth diagrams and vowel chart. It would be helpful to spend some time at the beginning of the course showing students how to interpret and use them. Note that the mouth diagrams are depicted in an appendix on page 97.

Audio Program

A multi-cassette audio program contains all of the listening material teachers will need to structure a dynamic aural/oral skills program. A sample cassette is available upon request.

unit 1

It's Not Miss.
It's Ms.

In this unit you will practice: final /s/ /z/ (*Miss/Ms.*)

Pronunciation Tool
See page 98.

Before you begin: Discuss the following questions with your classmates.

◆ In the United States, people have different formal titles: Dr., Mr., Miss, Ms., Mrs. Which of these titles could be used for the man?

◆ Which could be used for the woman?

A. **Read the questions. Then listen to the conversation and answer them.**

1. Who are the speakers?
   a. two men
   b. a man and a woman
   c. two women

2. Where are they?
   a. in Dr. Baines's office
   b. at work
   c. at home

3. What is the woman's name?
   a. Miss Cruz
   b. Mrs. Cruz
   c. Ms. Cruz

4. What does the man call her?
   a. Miss Cruz
   b. Mrs. Cruz
   c. Ms. Cruz

B. Listen and repeat these words.

s	z
this	is
thanks	he's
yes	she's
class	Ms.
office	please
six	where's
Miss	Baines

Look at the words below. Then listen to the conversation again. Is the final sound in each word *s* or *z* ? Make a check (√) for each word.

		s	z
1.	where's	_____	_____
2.	Dr. Baines	_____	_____
3.	Miss	_____	_____
4.	Ms.	_____	_____
5.	he's	_____	_____
6.	his	_____	_____
7.	office	_____	_____
8.	what's	_____	_____
9.	six	_____	_____
10.	thanks	_____	_____

C. Listen to the conversation and write the missing words in the blanks.

PEDRO: _____ that?

BILL: _____ Elvira._____ a guard.

PEDRO: _____ Mr. Matthews?

BILL: _____ in the laboratory.

PEDRO: _____ _____ six?

BILL: No, _____ seven.

D. **Listen to these numbers and repeat them.**

one	six	eleven	sixteen
two	seven	twelve	seventeen
three	eight	thirteen	eighteen
four	nine	fourteen	nineteen
five	ten	fifteen	twenty

Listen and write the numbers you hear.

a. _____ b. _____ c. _____

d. _____ e. _____ f. _____

g. _____ h. _____

E. **Ana Cruz is giving Ken Matthews some telephone numbers. Listen to the conversation and write the numbers on the correct lines.**

Guard's office _____   Ana Cruz's office _____

Dr. Jurgens's office _____   Ana Cruz's home _____
home _____

F. **Ask five classmates for their telephone numbers and write them down.**

Name	Telephone Number
1. _____	_____
2. _____	_____
3. _____	_____
4. _____	_____
5. _____	_____

unit *2*

Sam Zednick, Please.

Pronunciation Tool
See page 98.

In this unit you will practice: initial /s/ /z/ (*Sue/zoo*)

Before you begin: Discuss the following question with your classmates.

◆   What does a receptionist do?

A.   **Read the questions. Then listen to the conversation and answer them.**

1. Who are the speakers?
    a. two men
    b. two women
    c. a man and a woman

2. Where are they?
    a. in the office
    b. on the phone
    c. in a laboratory

3. What is the conversation about?
    a. a movie
    b. an experiment
    c. a scientist

B. Listen and repeat these words.

s	z
sink	zinc
Sue	zoo
seal	zeal
sip	zip

Sometimes words are spelled with an *s* but sound like *z*. Listen to these words. Circle the ones that have a *z* sound.

1. Susan   3. secret   5. test

2. sorry   4. thousand   6. visitor

Listen to the sentences. Write *s* or *z* in the blanks.

1. A _____ oologist is a kind of scientist.

2. The symbol for _____ ero is 0.

3. _____ eals are animals.

4. A _____ oo is a place for animals.

5. There is a _____ ink in the kitchen.

6. _____ inc is a kind of metal.

7. My sister's name is _____ usan.

Listen to each line of the conversation and repeat it.

ZACK: Sam Zednick, please.
OPERATOR: Sam Zednick the scientist?
ZACK: Yes, the zoologist.
OPERATOR: I'm sorry. He isn't here.
ZACK: Is his assistant, Zoe Slade, there?
OPERATOR: I'm sorry, she isn't. Can I take a message?
ZACK: Yes. Please tell Dr. Zednick that Zack Simpson called from Central Language School.

C. Listen to the letters of the alphabet and repeat them.

A B C D E F G H I J K L M

N O P Q R S T U V W X Y Z

Word Puzzles: Write the letters you hear. Then spell words with the letters. Follow the example.

1. e - r - b - a - z _____   1. zebra _____

2. _____   2. _____

3. _____   3. _____

4. _____   4. _____

D. **Listen to the conversation. Write *is*, *she's*, or *isn't* in the blanks.**

OPERATOR: Good morning, Central Language School.

ZOE SLADE: Good morning. _____ Zack Simpson there, please?

OPERATOR: No, Mr. Simpson _____ here this morning.

ZOE SLADE: _____ his assistant there?

OPERATOR: Yes, she _____, but she _____ in her office.

ZOE SLADE: Well, where _____ she?

OPERATOR: _____ in the language laboratory. There _____ no phone there

Who _____ this, please?

ZOE SLADE: This _____ Zoe Slade from Zenith. Z-E-N-I-T-H Incorporated.

OPERATOR: What _____ your phone number?

ZOE SLADE: 876-3459.

OPERATOR: Thank you. Mr. Simpson will call you tomorrow.

Listen to the conversation again and fill out the message form.

```
┌─────────────────────────────────────────────┐
│  For _____ │
│  Date _____Time _____          │
│       WHILE YOU WERE OUT                       │
│  M_____    │
│  From_____    │
│  Phone No. _____    │
│          Area Code    Number    Extension      │
│  ┌──────────────────┬──────────────────────┬─┐ │
│  │ TELEPHONED       │ URGENT               │ │ │
│  │ PLEASE CALL      │ WANTS TO SEE YOU     │ │ │
│  │ WILL CALL AGAIN  │ CAME TO SEE YOU      │ │ │
│  │ RETURNED YOUR CALL                      │ │ │
│  └──────────────────┴──────────────────────┴─┘ │
│  Message_____   │
│  _____  │
│  _____  │
│  _____  │
│                              Operator           │
└─────────────────────────────────────────────┘
```

E. Role Play. Follow the instructions below.

STUDENT A: You call Central Language School. You want to speak to Sandra Zanofsky.

STUDENT B: You work at Central Language School. Sandra Zanofsky isn't at work today. Complete the message form.

Now change roles.

STUDENT B: You call Central Language School. You want to speak to Sara Zimco.

STUDENT A: You work at Central Language School. Sara Zimco isn't at work today. Complete the message form.

For _____

Date _____Time_____

WHILE YOU WERE OUT

M_____

From_____

Phone No. _____

Area Code   Number   Extension

TELEPHONED		URGENT	
PLEASE CALL		WANTS TO SEE YOU	
WILL CALL AGAIN		CAME TO SEE YOU	
RETURNED YOUR CALL			

Message_____

_____

_____

_____

Operator

unit 3

My Daughter's a Lawyer.

In this unit you will practice: final /ər/ (*teacher*)

Before you begin: Discuss the following questions with your classmates.

◆ What are the occupations of these people?

◆ What other occupations can you name?

A. **Read the questions. Then listen to the conversation and answer them.**

1. Who are the speakers?
   a. mother and daughter
   b. sisters
   c. friends

2. The woman is talking about her
   a. friend's children.
   b. adult children.
   c. grandchildren.

3. Match the occupations with the names.

   Betty   actor

   Jim   writer

   Sue   lawyer

   Bill   doctor

B. Listen to these words.

teacher	visitor	sister	daughter	doctor
mother	brother	father	number	Heather
writer	baker	afternoon	fever	

Listen to the conversation. Circle the words that you hear in the list above.

Listen to the words again and repeat them.

Listen and repeat these sentences.

1. Heather's her daughter.

2. My mother's a writer.

3. Her brother has a fever.

4. My sister is a baker.

5. What's the doctor's number?

C. Words have sound groups (syllables). Some words have one syllable. Others have two or three or more. Listen to these words:

1 syllable	2 syllables	3 syllables
name	of/fice	tel/e/phone
six	num/ber	Wash/ing/ton
where's	morn/ing	sci/en/tist

Listen to the sentences. How many syllables do these words have? Write the words in the chart. Choose the correct column for each word.

1. daughter
2. carrier
3. December
4. you're
5. visitor

6. aren't
7. aren't
8. what's
9. When're
10. Who're

1 syllable	2 syllables	3 syllables
	daughter	

Say the words aloud.

D. **Listen for the words *are* and *aren't*. Also listen for *'re* at the end of words. Write *are, aren't,* or *'re* in the blanks below.**

POLICE OFFICER: Excuse me. _____ you lost?

MAN: Yes we _____, officer. We _____ New Yorkers. We _____ visitors.

POLICE OFFICER: Where _____ you going?

MAN: We _____ going to the World Trade Center.

POLICE OFFICER: That's easy. You _____ far from there. Just walk three blocks that way.

E. **Listen and repeat the names of these occupations.**

teacher	taxi driver	mail carrier	writer
baker	waiter	police officer	actor
doctor	singer	butcher	lawyer

Listen to the clues and name the occupation. You need to know these words: *uniform, carry, give.*

Occupation

1. Maria _____

2. Frank _____

3. Tania _____

Choose an occupation that you know about. Think of three or four clues that describe the occupation. Tell your partner each clue. Your partner will try to guess the occupation.

unit **4**

I Think That's Wrong.

In this unit you will practice: /θ/ (*thin*)

Pronunciation Tool
Pronunciation Tool **See page 98.**

Before you begin: Discuss the following question with your classmates.

◆ How much do a hamburger and a soft drink cost where you live?

A. **Read the questions. Then listen to the conversation and answer them.**

1. Where does this conversation take place?
   a. in a restaurant
   b. at work
   c. at home

2. What does Beth order?
   a. a hamburger
   b. a Coke
   c. a hamburger and a Coke

3. How much does it cost?
   a. $2.70
   b. $2.17
   c. $.27

B. **Listen and repeat these words.**

think	thin	thanks	math
thirsty	thing	path	bath

Listen and repeat these sentences.

1. I think they're thirsty.
2. Thanks for those things.
3. Your math book is in the bathroom.
4. She's thin.
5. Mr. Matthews is on the path.

C. **Some syllables in English are longer than others. Listen to these examples.**

wonderful   nationality   quiet   computer

Now listen to these words and draw a line under the longest syllable.

show/er	um/brel/la	col/or	ex/per/i/ment
o/kay	bed/room	o/range	na/tion/al/i/ty

Listen and repeat these numbers.

thirteen	fourteen	fifteen	sixteen	seventeen
eighteen	nineteen	twenty	thirty	forty
fifty	sixty	seventy	eighty	ninety

Listen to these numbers and draw a line under the longest syllable.

for/ty	four/teen
six/ty	six/teen
eigh/ty	eigh/teen

Listen and circle the number you hear.

1. seventy   seventeen
2. thirty   thirteen
3. fifty   fifteen
4. sixty   sixteen

D. **Listen to this conversation and fill in the numbers.**

A: Can you type?

B: Yes, about _____ words a minute.

A: That's great. My secretary can't type more than _____ .

B: How much can you pay me?

A: Only _____ an hour.

B: I can't work for less than _____ .

A: That's a problem. I can only spend _____ a week. How many hours can you work?

B: _____ .

A: OK. I can pay you _____ for _____ hours a week.

E. **Listen to the conversation and fill in the prices in the advertisement.**

DADE'S *SUMMER SALE*

Women's dresses $ _____ to $ _____

All summer shoes $ _____

SPECIAL IMPORTED ITALIAN SHOES $ _____

Blouses $ _____

Scarves $_____

F. **How much does a pizza cost? Discuss your ideas with one or more classmates. Then complete this menu for a pizza parlor.**

Pizza Palace

Pizza	**Drinks**
Plain: _____	Soft drinks: _____
One topping: _____	Milk: _____
Two toppings: _____	Juice: _____
Three toppings: _____	
Superextravaganza (6 toppings): _____	

Your partner will call and order some food. Take the order and tell your partner how much he or she will have to pay.

unit 5

Is That Their Thesaurus?

In this unit you will practice: /ð/ (*the*)

Pronunciation Tool
See page 98.

Before you begin: Discuss the following questions with your classmates.

♦ Do you use a dictionary? What can you find in a dictionary?

♦ What is a thesaurus? What can you find there?

A. **Read the questions. Then listen to the conversation and answer them.**

1. What are the names of the two people speaking?

   _____

2. What is the woman looking for?

   _____

3. Where is it?

   _____

B. **Listen and repeat these words.**

this	that	these	those	the
they	there	their	another	then

Listen and repeat these sentences.

1. They're in the room.
2. That's not their class.
3. This is another book.
4. There they go.
5. Those clothes are theirs.

   NOTE: *Clothes* is pronounced like *cloze*.

C. **Listen to these words. How many syllables do they have? Check (√) the correct column below.**

	1 syllable	2 syllables	3 syllables	4 syllables
1. meet	✓	_____	_____	_____
2. doctor	_____	_____	_____	_____
3. later	_____	_____	_____	_____
4. from	_____	_____	_____	_____
5. visitor	_____	_____	_____	_____
6. twelve	_____	_____	_____	_____
7. you're	_____	_____	_____	_____
8. assistant	_____	_____	_____	_____
9. conversation	_____	_____	_____	_____

D. **In fast speech, some words lose their *th* sound. Listen to the questions. Write the *th* words you hear.**

1. _____   4. _____
2. _____   5. _____
3. _____

Now listen to the questions again and repeat them.

E. Listen to the conversation. Then listen again. Next to each item, write the name of the person who owns it. There are three people: Brenda, John, and Ali. Say where each item is.

F. Role Play. Follow the instructions below.

STUDENT A: You are Thad. You can't find your math book. You think that Theodora has it. Ask her about it.

STUDENT B: You are Theodora. Thad can't find his math book. He thinks that you have it. You know that the math book you have is yours.

Can I Leave on Tuesday?

Pronunciation Tool
See page 99.

In this unit you will practice: /ə/ /æ/ (*can/can't*)

Before you begin: Discuss the following questions with your classmates.

◆ What are the advantages of traveling by plane?

◆ What are the disadvantages?

A. **Read the questions. Then listen to the conversation and answer them.**

1. Who is Mr. Black speaking to?
    a. his boss
    b. his wife
    c. a travel agent

2. What time does he leave? _____

3. What time does he arrive in New Orleans? _____

4. Can he leave on Tuesday? _____

B. **Can you hear the difference between** *can* **and** *can't* **? Listen to these sentences.**

1. I can go.

2. I can't go.

Which one has a longer vowel sound?

Now listen to this conversation. Write the word *can* **or** *can't* **in the blanks.**

TRAVEL AGENT: Ms. Conway, this is Lisa at Easy Travel. I'm calling about your travel arrangements.

MS. CONWAY: Thank you. _____ I leave on Friday night?

TRAVEL AGENT: I'm sorry. You _____ leave on Friday night. There are no more seats.

MS. CONWAY: Hmm. _____ I leave on Saturday morning?

TRAVEL AGENT: Yes, you _____ leave on Saturday, but you _____ fly direct to Minneapolis. You have to stop in Chicago.

MS. CONWAY: Well _____ I be in Minneapolis before 12? I'm going to a wedding, and I _____ be late.

TRAVEL AGENT: Oh dear. You won't arrive in Minneapolis until 2 P.M. What time is the wedding?

MS. CONWAY: 2:30.

TRAVEL AGENT: Well, _____ you leave on Friday afternoon?

MS. CONWAY: I _____ leave then. I have an important meeting at 3.

TRAVEL AGENT: _____ you change the meeting?

MS. CONWAY: I _____ try.

C. **Listen and repeat the days of the week.**

| Monday | Wednesday | Friday | Sunday |
| Tuesday | Thursday | Saturday | |

Listen and write the day of the week that you hear.

1. _____

2. _____

3. _____

4. _____

5. _____

6. _____

7. _____

D. **Listen to the conversation and complete the chart.**

from	to	flight number	time	days

E. **Role Play. Follow the instructions below.**

STUDENT A: Complete this chart. You are a travel agent. Student B calls you to make reservations from Chicago to Portland, Oregon.

from	to	flight number	time	days
Chicago	Portland			

STUDENT B: Call Student A and ask about flights from Chicago to Portland, Oregon.

Now change roles.

STUDENT B: Complete this chart. You are a travel agent. Student A calls you to make reservations from Miami to Denver, Colorado.

from	to	flight number	time	days
Miami	Denver			

STUDENT A: Call Student B and ask about flights from Miami to Denver.

unit 7

Congratulations, Pedro!

Pronunciation Tool
See page 97.

In this unit you will practice: /f/ /p/ (*fan/pan*)

Before you begin: Discuss the following questions with your classmates.

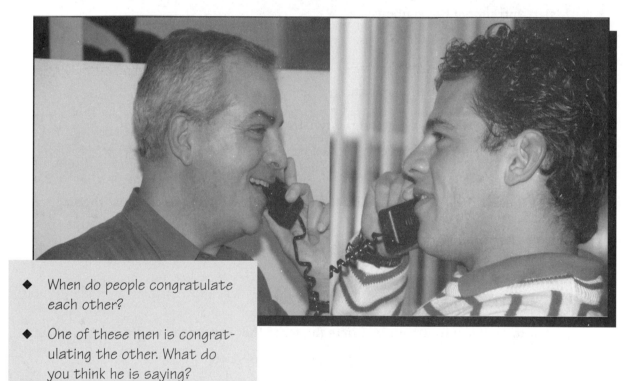

◆ When do people congratulate each other?

◆ One of these men is congrat-ulating the other. What do you think he is saying?

A.   Read the questions. Then listen to the conversation and answer them.

1. The two men are
   a. brothers.
   b. friends.
   c. father and son.

2. Who's Pat?
   a. the new mother
   b. the sister
   c. the baby

3.   What's the baby's name?

   _____

B. Listen and repeat the pairs of words.

past	fast
pig	fig
pin	fin
pile	file
pork	fork
pull	full
pea	fee
pear	fare

Listen and repeat the sentences.

Paul fell in a pile of peaches.

Get a fork full of pork.

That's Penny's perfumed pen.

Listen and try to repeat this tongue twister.

Peter Piper picked a peck of pickled peppers.

C. All of these words are stressed on the first syllable. Listen and repeat them.

•	•	•
morn/ing	bath/room	for/mu/la

•	•	•
mu/sic	can/dy	dan/ger/ous

Listen to each group of words. Circle the word that is stressed on the first syllable.

1. ex/per/i/ment   res/er/va/tion   mil/lion

2. phar/ma/cist   me/chan/ic   un/der/stand

3. cig/a/rette   riv/er   re/mem/ber

4. ma/chine   down/stairs   gov/ern/ment

5. caf/e/te/ri/a   tel/e/phone   wel/come

D. All of these words are stressed on the second syllable. Listen and repeat them.

       •   •   •   •   •

along   experiment   computer   pajamas   experience

Listen to each group of words. Circle the word that is stressed on the second syllable.

1. extra   supermarket   direction
2. remember   violent   person
3. building   select   perfect
4. police   sailor   mountain
5. lousy   comedy   terrific

E. Listen to the conversations and decide which card to send to each person.

_____

_____

_____

F. Imagine that today is a special day for you. Tell your partner. He or she will congratulate you.

unit 8

It's Your Turn to Wash the Dishes!

In this unit you will practice: final /ʃ/ /tʃ/ (*wash/watch*)

> **Pronunciation Tool**
> **See page 98.**

Before you begin: Discuss the following question with your classmates.

◆ Who does the dishes in your house?

A. **Read the questions. Then listen to the conversation and answer them.**

1. Who washes the dishes?_____

2. What else does Manuel do?_____

3. Who does the work in Cindy's house?_____

B. **Listen to these pairs of words.**

     1. wash   watch

     2. cash   catch

     3. dish   ditch

Now listen again and repeat each word.

Listen and circle the word you hear.

     1. cash   catch

     2. wash   watch

     3. dish   ditch

Listen and write the missing word in each blank.

     1. I can't pay you. I have no _____.

     2. Please _____ my _____.

     3. The police can't _____ all terrorists.

     4. Please tell me the time. I don't have my _____.

Now listen again and repeat each sentence.

C. **S has three different sounds at the ends of words. Listen to these words.**

	/s/	/z/	/ɛz/
1.	hats	pajamas	addresses
2.	kicks	rains	catches
3.	Philip's	Susan's	Joyce's

Listen to these words. Check (√) the sound you hear.

		/s/	/z/	/ɛz/
1.	cashes	___	___	___
2.	waits	___	___	___
3.	fixes	___	___	___
4.	pays	___	___	___
5.	keeps	___	___	___
6.	addresses	___	___	___
7.	sweaters	___	___	___
8.	offices	___	___	___
9.	sports	___	___	___
10.	Peter's	___	___	___
11.	Pat's	___	___	___
12.	Alex's	___	___	___

D. **Listen to this conversation and repeat each line.**

A: Is Butch there, Carol?

B: No, he isn't. He finishes work at 5. Maybe he's at Alex's.

A: Who's Alex?

B: A man he works with. They're good friends. He goes there a lot.

A: Please tell him to call me.

B: Sure. He comes home before 8. He always watches the sports news then.

Now practice the conversation with a classmate.

E. **Listen to the conversation and fill out the work schedule. Use the words below.**

vacuum   empty the trash   wash the dishes

iron   do the laundry   wash the kitchen floor

	Alex	Carol	Mike
Monday			wash the dishes
Tuesday			
Wednesday			
Thursday			
Friday			
Saturday			
Sunday			

F. **Who does these things in your household? Tell your partner.**

vacuum

empty the trash

do the laundry

iron

wash the dishes

cook

set the table

Queensland's Not in Kuwait!

In this unit you will practice: /kw/ (*quiz*)

Before you begin: Discuss the following question with your classmates.

◆ What do you study in geography?

A. Read the questions. Then listen to the conversation and answer them.

1. Who's speaking?
   a. a student and a teacher
   b. two teachers
   c. two students

2. Where are they?
   a. in a cafeteria
   b. in a library
   c. in a park

3. When does their class start?
   a. 2:30
   b. 2:00
   c. 2:15

4. Where is Queensland?
   a. in Canada
   b. in Kuwait
   c. in Australia

B. **Listen and repeat these words.**

quiet   quit   question   quarter   queen   quiz   quote

Listen and repeat these sentences.

1. Question the queen quickly.
2. The ducks quacked quite quietly.
3. He quit the quartet.
4. He read the notes quickly.

C. **These words are stressed on the third syllable. Listen and repeat them.**

•   •   •   •

e/lec/tri/ci/ty u/ni/ver/si/ty na/tion/al/i/ty res/er/va/tion

Listen to each group of words. Circle the word that is stressed on the third syllable.

1. ap/pli/ca/tion ex/pen/sive sud/den/ly
2. an/y/thing man/u/fac/ture ter/mi/nal
3. prob/a/bly sec/re/tar/y com/pre/hen/sion
4. fas/cin/ate ec/o/nom/ic won/der/ful
5. mag/a/zine to/mor/row ab/so/lute/ly

D. **Brenda didn't go to school today. She's calling her friend Margo to get some information about her classes. Listen to the conversation and fill in the blanks in Brenda's notebook.**

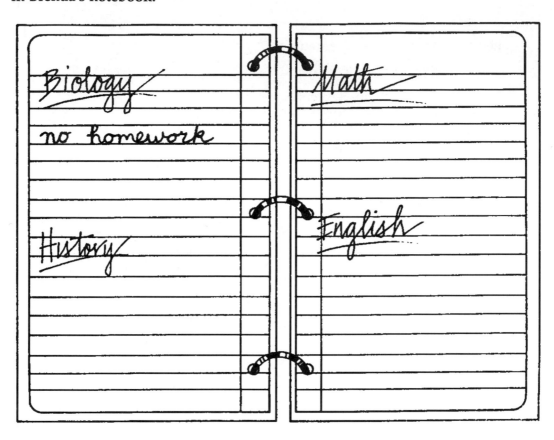

E. **Tell about it. Follow the instructions below.**

STUDENT A: Tell your partner what you did on the weekend.
STUDENT B: Listen and take notes.

Now change roles.

Review

A.   **Listen to these words. Then check (√) the column for the number of syllables you *hear*.**

	1 syllable	2 syllables	3 syllables	4 syllables
1. reference	_____	_____	_____	_____
2. business	_____	_____	_____	_____
3. watched	_____	_____	_____	_____
4. conversation	_____	_____	_____	_____
5. permission	_____	_____	_____	_____

B.   **Listen and write *can* or *can't* in each blank.**

1. We _____ go to school today.

2. You _____ leave early.

3. Carol _____ drive a car.

4. _____ I go now?

Now listen again and repeat the sentences.

C.   **Listen and write the letters you hear.**

1. _____

2. _____

3. _____

4. _____

Now unscramble the words.

D. **Listen and write the sentences.**

1. _____

2. _____

3. _____

4. _____

E. **LISTENING BINGO: This bingo board contains words. Cross out each word you hear. When you complete a horizontal line or a vertical line, you have bingo.**

B	I	N	G	O
can't	wash	bath	turn	zeal
hiss	cash	stay	catch	who's
dime	sink	miss	who	vine
seal	fan	watch	say	Ms.
thin	where's	dish	home	hat

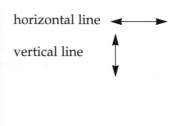

horizontal line

vertical line

unit **11**

Watch the Curve, Phil!

Pronunciation Tool
See page 97.

In this unit you will practice: /f/ /v/ (*few/view*)

Before you begin: Discuss the following questions with your classmates.

◆ Do you drive?

◆ Are you a good driver?

A. **Read the questions. Then listen to the conversation and answer them.**

1. Where are the speakers?
   a. at home
   b. on a picnic
   c. in a car

2. What does Phil like?
   a. the view
   b. the car
   c. the curves

3. Vera is worried about
   a. the view.
   b. the leaves.
   c. the curves.

B. Listen and repeat these words.

Vera	never	of
view	over	drive
very	lover	have
van	giving	gave

Listen and repeat these words and phrases.

few	safer	off
fast	have to	cliff
fat	lift	leaf
fur	sofa	half

Listen and repeat these sentences.

1. Does Vera have a fan?
2. Do I have to drive very fast?
3. He gave Phil a few vans.
4. Don't drive off the cliff.
5. What kind of fur is that?

C. Words in English have a tune, like a song. Sometimes the tune goes down like steps.

ahead

Sometimes the tune goes down like a hill.

nine

Sometimes the tune goes up.

no?

Listen to the tune of these words.

yes   bluejeans   pajamas   cafeteria   ahead

Listen to these words and draw lines to show the tune.

1. no
2. sorry
3. another
4. laboratory
5. divorced

Listen and repeat the dialogue.

    A: Look!

    B: Where?

    A: There.

    B: There?

    A: No, there.

    B: Oh, I see.

Now practice it with another classmate.

D. **Vera is a good driver, but Phil isn't. Listen to the conversation and circle the things that Phil ignored.**

a *Stop* sign	a traffic light	a *Bump Ahead* sign
a *Keep Right* sign	a school zone speed limit	a *Dangerous Curve Ahead* sign

E. **Role Play. Follow the instructions below.**

STUDENT A: You think you are a good driver but Student B keeps criticizing your driving. Argue with him or her but remember to keep your eyes on the road.

STUDENT B: You are a passenger in Student A's car. He or she is not a very careful driver. Give him or her some advice.

My Dog Was Chewing My New Shoe!

In this unit you will practice initial: /ʃ/ /tʃ/ (*shoe/chew*)

**Pronunciation Tool
See page 98.**

Before you begin: Discuss the following questions with your classmates.

- ◆ Do you like dogs?

- ◆ How do dogs sometimes cause trouble?

A. Read the questions. Then listen to the conversation and answer them.

1. What was Chuck doing?
   a. shaving
   b. shouting
   c. chewing

2. What was Chuck's dog doing?
   a. shaving
   b. shouting
   c. chewing

3. What does Sherry think that Chuck should get?
   a. a new dog
   b. new shoes
   c. a dog bone

B. **Listen and repeat these pairs of words.**

chin	shin
chew	shoe
cheese	she's
chip	ship
chop	shop
cheap	sheep
cheat	sheet

Listen and repeat these sentences.

1. Please change the channel and choose a good show.

2. They chose shrimp and cheese from Chuck's shop.

3. You should check the shirt.

C. **Listen to these yes/no questions. Does the tune go up or down at the end? Draw lines to show the tune.**

1. Is Vera a student?

2. Do they have to leave?

3. Does he live here?

4. Can you speak English very well?

5. Are they driving fast?

Listen and repeat these questions.

1. Are you from this city?

2. Do you have brothers and sisters?

3. Do you like English?

4. Can you cook?

5. Do you work?

Now ask a classmate the questions.

D. **Dictation. You will hear the dictation three times. The first time, listen only. The second time, write. The third time, check your work. When you hear the word *period*, write "." at the end of the sentence.**

_____

_____

_____

_____

_____

E. **Use your imagination to make up a silly story. Then tell your story to your partner.**

STUDENT A: Try to use these words: sheep, shop, change, shut, choose, shampoo, shock.

STUDENT B: Try to use these words: shelf, shape, chart, show, cheat, short, chair.

Help! It's an Emergency!

Pronunciation Tool
See page 98.

In this unit you will practice: /dʒ / /tʃ/ (*Jane/chain*)

Before you begin: Discuss the following question with your classmates.

◆ Why do you think the woman in the picture is dialing an emergency number?

A. **Read the questions. Then listen to the conversation and answer them.**

   1. The two people who are talking
      a. are good friends.
      b. don't know each other.
      c. are brother and sister.

2. The woman acts
   a. excited.
   b. calm.
   c. upset.

3. The woman was in a _____ accident.
   a. car
   b. boat
   c. train

4. The woman was
   a. alone.
   b. with another woman.
   c. with a man.

B. **Listen and repeat these words.**

Japan	jeans	Jane	George
page	college	edge	schedule

Now listen to these words. Check (√) the column of the sound you hear.

	j	*ch*
1.	_____	_____
2.	_____	_____
3.	_____	_____
4.	_____	_____
5.	_____	_____
6.	_____	_____

Listen to this dialogue and fill in the blanks with *ch* or *j*.

A: Can I take your order?

B: Yes. I'd _____ ust like _____ am and _____ eese, please.

A: _____ am and _____ eese? Are you _____ oking?

B: No. I'd like a _____ am and _____ eese sandwich and a large glass of orange _____ uice.

A: Anything else?

B: Yes, _____ erry _____ uice and _____ icken for my _____ ild. And _____ arge it to my account, please.

Now listen again and repeat the dialogue.

C. **Listen to these sentences and write *is*, *are*, *was*, or *were* in the blanks.**

1. George _____ here.

2. Jane _____ alone.

3. The children _____ on schedule.

4. They _____ dangerous men.

5. Who _____ in college?

6. Where _____ you?

Now listen again and repeat the sentences.

D. **Listen to the intonation of the underlined words.**

1. He wants <u>milk</u>.　　　He wants <u>milk</u>, <u>toast</u>, and <u>cereal</u>.

2. He teaches <u>Doreen</u>.　　He teaches <u>Doreen</u>, <u>Cathy</u>, and <u>Mike</u>.

Which words go up? Which words go down?

Now listen and repeat these sentences.

1. We have vacation in June, July, and August.

2. I have to work Monday, Tuesday, and Wednesday.

3. Let me count them. One, two, three, four, five.

4. Please buy peas, carrots, and lettuce.

E. **Listen to the call to Emergency Line and fill out this form. Choose the right information from the list below.**

EMERGENCY REPORT

1. TIME OF CALL: _____

2. CALLER: _____

3. TYPE OF EMERGENCY: _____

4. DETAILS: _____

5. PLACE OF EMERGENCY: _____

6. TYPE OF HELP NEEDED: _____

1.	11:15	**3.**	car accident	**5.**	Chainbridge Road
	11:55		boat accident		Jamesbridge Road
2.	George Charles	**4.**	a car and a truck	**6.**	police
	James Charles		a car and a van		police and ambulance

F. **Role Play. Follow the instructions below.**

STUDENT A: Call to report an emergency.
STUDENT B: You work at Emergency Line. Take Student A's phone call and make notes to complete an emergency report.

EMERGENCY REPORT

1. TIME OF CALL: _____

2. CALLER: _____

3. TYPE OF EMERGENCY: _____

4. DETAILS: _____

5. PLACE OF EMERGENCY: _____

6. TYPE OF HELP NEEDED: _____

Now change roles.

We Waited 12 Hours for Tickets.

In this unit you will practice: final /p/ /t/ /k/ /b/ /d/ /g/
(*rope/get/look/bib/bead/cog*)

Before you begin: Discuss the following questions with your classmates.

◆ Have you ever heard Mariah Carey sing?

◆ What singers do you like?

A. **Read the questions. Then listen to the conversation and answer them.**

1. Who are Kate and Barb?
   a. friends
   b. sisters
   c. roommates

2. Who bought the tickets?
   a. Kate and Nick
   b. Kate and Barb
   c. Barb and Nick

3. Who asked Mary to work?
   a. Kate did.
   b. Nick did.
   c. Barb did.

B. Listen to these words and number them in the order you hear them.

_____ cab _____ cad _____ cap _____ cat

Now listen to these words and number them in the order you hear them.

_____ kit _____ kick _____ kid _____ Kip

Now listen and repeat these words.

road   get   wait   Bob   ride   look   sleep

good   week   up   bib   cog   wake   bug

Listen to the sentences. Fill in the blanks with the correct words.

1. The _____ can't play in the _____.

2. You can't _____ here.

3. Don't _____ your _____.

4. Give _____ the _____.

Now listen again and repeat the sentences.

C. Listen to these pairs. Write the number of syllables in each word.

			number of syllables					number of syllables
1.	present	kick	_____	5.	present	add	_____
	past	kicked	_____		past	added	_____
2.	present	wait	_____	6.	present	fill	_____
	past	waited	_____		past	filled	_____
3.	present	need	_____	7.	present	laugh	_____
	past	needed	_____		past	laughed	_____
4.	present	watch	_____	8.	present	paint	_____
	past	watched	_____		past	painted	_____

Which verbs added a syllable in the past tense?

_____   _____   _____   _____

Complete this rule.

When the present form of a verb ends in _____ or _____, the past tense has an extra syllable.

Pronounce the past tense of these verbs.

rent	close	fade	use	start
wash	paint	intend	wait	watch
kick				

D. **Yes/no questions and *wh*-questions have different tunes. Listen to these questions.**

Is he old?   How old is he?

Now listen and repeat these questions.

1. Do you study?
2. When do you study?
3. How do you turn on the television?
4. Is it Persian?
5. Do you usually stay home?
6. Where are they going?

E. **Listen to this conversation. Make notes about what Kim did last weekend.**

Who? _____

How? _____

Where? _____

What? _____

F. **Ask your partner questions about what he or she did last weekend.**

unit 15

Call the Police!

In this unit you will practice: /l/   /r/ (*lamp/ramp*)

Pronunciation Tool
See page 97.

Before you begin: **Discuss the following question with your classmates.**

◆ Why *do* you think this woman called the police?

$A.$ **Read the questions. Then listen to the conversation and answer them.**

1. What is the conversation about?
   a. a robbery
   b. an accident
   c. a library

2. The people speaking are
   a. two police officers.
   b. a police officer and a woman.
   c. a police officer and a robber.

3. What color hair did the man in the library have?
   a. red
   b. brown
   c. black

B. **Listen and repeat these words.**

lab	call	milk	ride	fire	large
like	pencil	help	radio	your	beard
leave	steal	hold	rock	door	work

Listen and circle the words you hear.

1. light   right   4. you'll   you're

2. long   wrong   5. later   rate her

3. file   fire   6. lamp   ramp

Now listen again and repeat the words.

Listen to the conversation and write the missing words in the blanks.

A: _____ me about _____ night.

B: _____, I was home _____, and I _____ a noise in

the _____.

A: What did you do?

B: I _____ to open the _____, but it was _____.

So I _____ in the window and saw a robber.

A: What did he _____ _____?

B: He was a _____ man with a _____ _____.

A: What did he _____?

B: My _____, my _____, and a _____ locket.

Now listen again and repeat the conversation.

C. **Listen to the questions and write *did he*, *did she*, or *did you* in the blanks.**

1. _____ see him?

2. _____ leave?

3. What _____ do?

4. Who _____ listen to?

5. Where _____ eat lunch?

Now listen again and repeat the questions.

D. Listen to the conversation. Then read the newspaper story. Underline the mistakes.

ROBBERY AT LOGAN CITY MUSEUM

There was a robbery at the Logan City Museum last night. The robbers stole many jewels including the Raja's diamond, which is worth 3 million dollars. Police believe that the robbers got in by breaking a window. The police say that the burglar alarm didn't go off because it wasn't working properly. The police say that the robbers are probably part of a group that travels around the world robbing museums.

E. Use your imagination to make up answers to these questions about a robbery. Your partner will ask you the questions to find out your answers.

1. Where did the robbery happen?

2. What time did the robbery happen?

3. How many robbers were there?

4. What did the robbers take?

5. Who called the police?

6. Did the police catch the robbers?

   If yes, how?

   If no, why not?

unit 16

Excuse Me, I'm Conducting a Survey.

In this unit you will practice: /h/ /f/ (*hill/fill*)

**Pronunciation Tool
See page 99.**

Before you begin: Discuss the following questions with your classmates.

◆ What is a survey?

◆ What questions might someone ask in a telephone survey?

A. **Read the questions. Then listen to the conversation and answer them.**

1. Where does this conversation take place?
   a. on the telephone
   b. in the street
   c. in Helen's office

2. Who's talking?
   a. Helen and a friend
   b. Helen and a stranger
   c. Helen and Harry

3. What are the questions about?
   a. work
   b. hobbies
   c. health

4. How often does Helen exercise?
   a. sometimes
   b. often
   c. never

B. **Listen and repeat these words.**

   hurry   help   health   hello   high

Listen and repeat these words.

   fair   funny   foot   first   food

Listen and circle the words you hear.

   1. hit   fit   **3.** her   fur   **5.** hair   fare
   2. his   fizz   **4.** home   foam   **6.** hat   fat

Listen to this conversation and fill in the missing words.

MARTHA: What are you doing, Harry?

HARRY: I'm _____ my _____ _____.

MARTHA: What? I can't _____ you.

HARRY: Let me turn _____ the _____.

MARTHA: How are you _____?

HARRY: Oh, I'm _____.

MARTHA: _____ told me you _____ your _____.

HARRY: Yes, but it's _____ now.

Now listen again and repeat the conversation.

C. Listen to the sentences and fill in the blanks with *him*, *her*, or *them*.

1. Give _____ the book.

2. I can't forget _____.

3. She smiles at _____.

4. Don't think about _____.

5. You can buy _____ a bathing suit.

D. Listen and repeat these past-tense verbs.

walked   called   looked   watched   laughed   smiled

worked   missed   stopped   learned   mixed   tried

Does the –ed sound the same for all the verbs?

Listen again and write each verb in the proper column, according to the pronunciation of –ed.

called	*kicked*	*needed*

Complete this rule.

When the present tense of a verb ends in a _____ or a _____ sound, we pronounce the –ed

like /ɪd/. If the present tense of a verb ends in any other sound, we pronounce the –ed like

_____ or _____.

E. Listen to the conversation and fill out this survey.

Survey				
	ALWAYS	USUALLY	SOMETIMES	NEVER
Eat breakfast?				
Make breakfast yourself?				
Coffee?				
Cereal?				
Eggs?				
Toast?				
Sausage?				
Bacon?				
Juice?				

F. Interview your partner and fill out this survey.

Survey				
	ALWAYS	USUALLY	SOMETIMES	NEVER
Eat breakfast?				
Make breakfast yourself?				
Coffee?				
Cereal?				
Eggs?				
Toast?				
Sausage?				
Bacon?				
Juice?				

unit 17

It's a Lovely Apartment.

In this unit you will practice: /v/ /b/ (*vote/boat*)

Before you begin: Discuss the following questions with your classmates.

◆ What are some advantages of living in a city?

◆ What are some of the disadvantages?

A. **Read the questions. Then listen to the conversation and answer them.**

1. Where do the speakers probably live?
   a. in a small town
   b. in a city
   c. in Boston

2. Who's moving?
   a. Vicky
   b. Vanessa
   c. both of them

3. Why doesn't Vicky like cities?
   a. She doesn't like the traffic.
   b. She thinks the people aren't friendly.
   c. She thinks there's too much violence.

4. Where does Vanessa want to live?
   a. near her friend Charles
   b. near the river
   c. in the center of the city

B. **Listen and repeat these words.**

vanilla	violent	very	every	love
adventure	reserve	over	river	

Circle the word you hear.

1. vie   buy
2. vote   boat
3. vow   bow
4. vet   bet
5. vest   best

Listen to these sentences and fill in the missing words.

1. Every berry is _____ good.

2. I _____ _____ adventure movies.

3. Wear your _____ _____.

Now listen again and repeat the sentences.

C. Listen to the questions and fill in the blanks with *did + he* or *she*.

1. _____ go?

2. Why _____ leave?

3. Who _____ see?

4. When _____ come back?

5. How _____ know?

D. Listen and repeat these phrases.

First syllable stress

1. háp/py   téach/er

2. yél/low   íce cream

First and second syllable stress

3. pré/fér   áp/plés

4. búr/glár   a/lárm

Second syllable stress

5. a/sléep   a/gáin

6. ar/ríve   be/fóre

Now listen to these pairs of phrases. Check *same* if they have the same stress pattern. Check *different* if they don't.

	same	different
1. forget to go money order	_____	_____
2. busy writer modern building	_____	_____
3. surprise party subtract money	_____	_____
4. pretty dirty early winter	_____	_____
5. mountain climber angry police	_____	_____

E. **Look at the apartment advertisement. Then listen to the conversation. Write the answers to the questions below.**

LOVELY ONE BEDROOM
   APARTMENT
MODERN BUILDING
VIEW OF RIVER
EAST BOSTON REALTY
555-4789

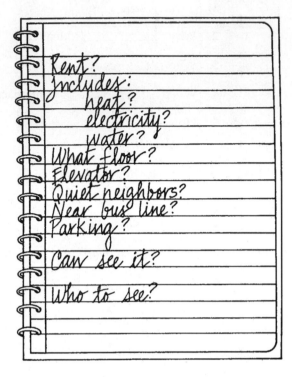

Rent?
Includes:
   heat?
   electricity?
   water?
What floor?
Elevator?
Quiet neighbors?
Near bus line?
Parking?

Can see it?

Who to see?

F. **Write an advertisement for an apartment. Show the advertisement to your partner. He or she will call and ask you questions about the apartment. Be sure to have your answers ready.**

unit **18**

You Cheated on the Test! No, I Studied!

In this unit you will practice: initial /t/ /tʃ/ (*test/chest*)

> **Pronunciation Tool**
> **See page 97.**

Before you begin: Discuss the following questions with your classmates.

◆ What do you think of people who cheat on tests?

◆ Is it ever OK to cheat?

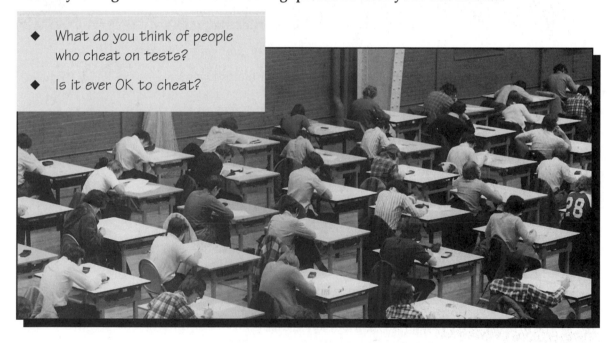

A. **Read the questions. Then listen to the conversation and answer them.**

1. The two people speaking are probably
   a. husband and wife.
   b. classmates.
   c. brother and sister.

2. What grade did Chuck get on the math test? _____

3. What grade did Tina get on the math test? _____

4. Why is Tina angry? _____

Listen and circle the words you hear.

1. tip   chip
2. tick   chick
3. till   chill
4. tin   chin

Now listen again and repeat the words.

Listen to these sentences and write the words you hear.

1. A _____ is a small bird.
2. It's made of _____ .
3. He hit his _____ .
4. Put the money in the _____ .
5. A _____ is a kind of insect.
6. Leave a _____ for the waitress.

C. **Sometimes we use stress to contradict an earlier statement.**

He went to Hawaii.   No, he didn't. He went to *Florida*.

Today's Jane's birthday.   No, her birthday's *tomorrow*.

Listen and underline the word with the most stress in the response.

1. Math is a lot easier than English.
   Are you kidding? English is much easier!

2. People in the United States can vote at 16.
   No. They can't vote until they're eighteen.

3. Canada has two official languages, English and Spanish.
   That's not right. Their official languages are English and French.

4. Just think. You only have two more semesters until you graduate.
   I wish! I have two more years.

Student A: Say these sentences to your partner. He or she will correct you.

1. Brazilians speak Spanish.
2. The sun revolves around the Earth.
3. There are 51 states in the United States.
4. Athens is the capital of Italy.

Student B: Say these sentences to your partner. He or she will correct you.

1. Dogs are smarter than cats.
2. Philadelphia is the capital of the United States.
3. India is in Europe.
4. Five times eight (5 x 8) equals forty-eight.

D. **The word *and* is sometimes pronounced *n*. Listen and repeat these phrases.**

> mother and father
>
> black and white
>
> night and day
>
> cats and dogs
>
> ham and eggs

The word *or* is sometimes pronounced *er*. Listen and repeat these phrases.

> tea or coffee
>
> north or south
>
> rainy or sunny
>
> here or there
>
> sister or brother

Listen and fill in the blanks with *and* or *or*.

1. You can have milk _____ juice.

2. Should we go to the beach _____ the movies?

3. Does he like Susan _____ Carol?

4. It's nice here summer _____ winter.

5. Do you want ham _____ cheese?

6. It's raining cats _____ dogs.*

*This means: it's raining a lot.

Now listen again and repeat the sentences.

E. **Choose a topic below and have a debate between two groups of students. One group will agree with the statement. The other will disagree. Each group should discuss the statements first.**

a. There should be no immigration laws. People should be able to live in any country they choose.

b. Education should follow strict rules. Traditional education is best.

c. There should be no limits on scientific experimentation.

Where Was Your Last Job?

Pronunciation Tool
See page 98.

In this unit you will practice: /y/ /dʒ/ (*your / job*)

Before you begin: Discuss the following questions with your classmates.

♦ Have you ever gone to a job interview?

♦ What questions might someone ask at a job interview?

A. **Read the statements. Then listen to the conversation. For each statement, write T for true or F for false.**

1. The two men are the same age. _____

2. The young man wants a job. _____

3. The job is at Johnson's Laboratory. _____

4. The older man wants to hire him. _____

5. The young man has a lot of experience. _____

6. The young man got an A in his computer course. _____

B. Listen and repeat these words.

yogurt	your	join
young	job	danger
yes	jam	page

Listen and circle the words you hear.

1. year jeer **3.** yaw jaw **5.** you Jew

2. yoke joke **4.** yet jet

Listen to this conversation and fill in the missing words.

A: I'd really like to _____ _____ company.

B: Well, there's a computer _____ that isn't filled _____.

A: Do _____ think I could get it?

B: _____. They're looking for _____ people like

_____.

A: How much does it pay a _____ ?

B: _____ should call Dr. _____ to find out.

C. The *y* sound of the words *you* and *your* often sounds like *j*. Listen to these questions. Fill in the blanks with *you* or *your*.

1. Did _____ eat?

2. Who did _____ hair?

3. When did _____ leave?

4. Where did _____ child go?

5. Whose car did _____ see?

Now listen again and repeat the questions.

D. **Listen to the conversation and fill in the blanks on the questionnaire. You will not be able to fill in all the blanks.**

```
┌─────────────────────────────────────────────────────────────────────┐
│                     CALLER INFORMATION CARD                           │
│  NAME _____        │
│  AGE _____        │
│  TYPE OF JOB _____        │
│  EXPERIENCE _____        │
│  EDUCATION _____        │
│       HIGH SCHOOL _____        │
│           YEAR OF GRADUATION _____        │
│       COLLEGE _____        │
│           YEAR OF GRADUATION _____        │
│  INTERVIEW     yes    no                                              │
│       TIME _____                         │
└─────────────────────────────────────────────────────────────────────┘
```

E. **Role Play. Follow the instructions below.**

STUDENT A: You own a small messenger company. You need a new messenger. Think about the qualifications of the person you want to hire and what your company can offer this person. Then interview Student B for the job.

skills and abilities needed
work experience
working hours
what salary you can offer
what benefits your company offers

STUDENT B: You apply to be a messenger in Student A's messenger company. Think about the things below and then convince Student A to hire you.

your work experience
how many hours a week you can work and when
what salary you want
what other benefits you want

Review

A. **Read the questions. Then listen to the conversation and answer them.**

1. Chris is talking to someone who is probably
   a. married.
   b. single.
   c. divorced.

2. The woman's name is
   a. Martha.
   b. Mary.
   c. Marion.

3. She is Chris's
   a. mother.
   b. friend.
   c. sister.

4. She wants to meet men who are interested in
   a. watching TV.
   b. the same things she is.
   c. her.

Listen again and check (√) the sentences you hear.

1. a. I'm going to a dating service.
   b. I'm going to go to a dating service.
   c. I'm going to go on a date.

2. a. I know, and I don't want to make a mistake.
   b. I know, but I can't make another mistake.
   c. I know, but I don't want to make another mistake.

3. a. How can you learn about a person from a piece of paper?
   b. What can you learn about a person from a piece of paper?
   c. Can you learn about a person from a piece of paper?

B. Listen to these sentences and write the missing words in the blanks.

1. I _____ sleep when I _____.

2. _____ cut his _____.

3. He was _____ a _____ _____.

4. _____ flew without _____ _____?

5. _____ the _____ near the _____ in the

   _____.

6. This _____ he got a _____ flying a _____.

Now listen again and repeat the sentences.

C. Listen to these sentences. Then draw lines to indicate the intonation. Follow the example.

1. Did Tom go to the store?

2. Where's she going?

3. We got milk, bread, cheese, and fish.

4. We forgot to buy fruit.

5. When are you coming home?

D. WORD BINGO: Listen to these words. Cross out each word you hear. When you complete a horizontal or vertical line, you have bingo.

B	I	N	G	O
Jew	yam	kid	best	chin
chip	queen	chew	tip	lamp
kick	fire	chill	tin	ramp
gin	vest	jam	cap	file
dripped	drip	green	kicked	rest

E. Look at these past-tense verbs. Listen to the sounds of their endings. Check (√) the column under the word that has the same ending sound. Follow the example.

	watched	called	tested
1. turned		√	
2. tied			
3. washed			
4. needed			
5. wanted			
6. danced			

F. Listen to these sentences and fill in the missing pronouns.

1. Did _____ eat?

2. Is _____ going?

3. Give _____ the book.

4. Take _____ to your teacher.

5. Make _____ leave early.

G. Listen to the conversation and fill in the form from the dating service.

Ideal Man

APPEARANCE

height _____ weight _____

eye color _____ hair color _____

PERSONALITY (circle correct adjectives)

kind   generous   affectionate   talkative   shy

INTERESTS

_____ _____ _____

POSSIBLE OCCUPATIONS

_____ _____ _____

---

unit 21

I'm Taking a Vacation.

In this unit you will practice: clear and unclear vowels

Before you begin: Discuss the following question with your classmates.

◆ Do you enjoy going to the beach? Why or why not?

A. **Read the questions. Then listen to the conversation and answer them.**

1. Where does this conversation take place?
   a. on the telephone
   b. in a store
   c. in Karen's home

2. Who are the speakers?
   a. Karen and Sue
   b. Mr. and Mrs. Baxter
   c. Karen and her mother

3. Who is taking a vacation?
   a. Sue
   b. Karen
   c. Mrs. Baxter

4. Where are Mr. and Mrs. Baxter going?
   a. to the store
   b. to the movies
   c. to a play

B. **Many vowels in English are not said clearly. Only the vowels in stressed syllables are clear or full. Listen to this word. It has three *a's*, but only one is said fully.**

   pa/já/mas

Now listen to this word. You can pronounce it with the accent on the first syllable or on the second syllable. Notice the difference in the pronunciation of the *a*.

   ad/dréss   ád /dress

Listen to these pairs of words and circle the clear vowel in each word.

1. reserve   reservation
2. invite   invitation
3. comedy   comedian
4. photograph   photography

Now listen again and repeat the words.

Some words in English look the same but are pronounced in different ways. Listen to these words. Circle the clear vowel in each word.

adjective	*noun*	*verb*
1. perfect		perfect
2.	present	present
3.	record	record
4.	object	object

Now listen again and repeat the words.

Sometimes an unstressed vowel is not pronounced at all and a syllable is lost. Listen to these words. Put an X over the vowel you don't hear.

1. interesting   3. temperature

2. comfortable   4. vegetable

C. **The *–ing to* in *going to* often sounds like *gonna*. Listen and repeat these sentences.**

1. She's going to leave.

2. They're going to study.

3. I'm going to work.

4. You're going to go.

5. He's going to dance.

D. **Listen to the conversation. Where are John and Maggie going on vacation? Write their travel plans.**

TRAVEL ITINERARY

Date	Leave	Arrive	Method of Transportation
May 10	Los Angeles	London	plane

E. **You're going to Europe for two weeks. Look at the map above and plan your vacation. Then tell your partner about your plans.**

What's for Dinner?

In this unit you will practice: /I/ /iʸ/ (chip/cheap)

**Pronunciation Tool
See page 99.**

Before you begin: Discuss the following questions with your classmates.

◆ Do you like food from other countries?

◆ What kinds of food do you like?

A. **Read the questions. Then listen to the conversation and put a check (√) under the name that correctly answers each question.**

	Bill	Tina	Joan
1. Who's hungry?	____	____	____
2. Who's going to Maria's?	____	____	____
3. Who likes Japanese food?	____	____	____
4. Who wants to eat hamburgers?	____	____	____
5. Who's going to eat Japanese food?	____	____	____
6. Who's going to eat Mexican food?	____	____	____

B.   **Listen to these words.**

	it	*eat*
1.	chip	cheap
2.	flit	fleet
3.	rich	reach

Listen and circle the words you hear.

1.	it	eat
2.	live	leave
3.	hill	heel
4.	ship	sheep

Now listen again and repeat the words.

Listen to these words and check (√) the sound you hear.

	it	*eat*
1.	_____	_____
2.	_____	_____
3.	_____	_____
4.	_____	_____

Listen and repeat these sentences.

1. Busy bees are pretty rich.
2. Give the cheese to Lynn.
3. We eat fish in April.

C.   **The letter *i* is usually pronounced like the *i* in *hill* and *rich* when it comes between two consonants or at the beginning of a word. Listen to these words:**

ink   in   big   did   him   kick   kitchen   kiss

Now listen and repeat these words.

chin   lick   kid   public   difficult   lift   important

D. Listen and repeat these questions with *going to.*

    1. Are you going to go?

    2. Is he going to leave?

    3. Who's going to teach?

    4. Where are you going to eat?

Listen and write these sentences.

    1. _____

    2. _____

    3. _____

    4. _____

E. Look at the reservation book below and listen to the conversations. Add information or make changes in the reservation book.

TIME	NAME	# OF PERSONS	TIME	NAME	# OF PERSONS
6:00	ANDERSON	2	7:00	KELLEHER	6
6:00	WANG	6	7:00	DECKER	4
6:00	JONES	2	7:00	SOLENSKY	2
6:00			7:00	GILLIES	2
6:00	VALDEZ	2	7:00	LYNCH	3
6:00	RAMSAY	4	7:00	GORALSKI	4
6:00	JOHNSON	2	7:00	HARRIS	4
6:30	HERNANDEZ	4	7:30	MARCONI	2
6:30	ATAMIAN	4	7:30	PETERSEN	2
6:30	McCARTHY	2	7:30		
6:30	SMITH	2	7:30	YUNG	2
6:30	POZINAK	4	7:30	DOOLEY	4
6:30	GOLDBERG	8	7:30	O'ROURKE	4
6:30			7:30	VAN VLIET	3

F. Role Play. Follow the instructions below.

    STUDENT A: Look at the reservation book for Akiko's Restaurant. Pretend you are one of the people. Call and change your reservation.

    STUDENT B: You work at Akiko's Restaurant. Answer Student A's phone call.

Now change roles.

unit 23

It's a Beautiful Island.

In this unit you will practice: /aɪ/ (*light*)

Before you begin: Discuss the following question with your classmates.

◆ Many people think that an island is a special place. Why?

A. **Read the questions. Then listen to the commercial and answer them.**

1. Where is Palm Island?
   a. in the Atlantic Ocean
   b. in the Pacific Ocean
   c. in the Gulf of Mexico

2. Which of these can you do on Palm Island?
   a. swim
   b. play tennis
   c. hike
   d. water ski

3. How far is Palm Island from New Orleans?
   a. 60 minutes
   b. 16 minutes
   c. 1 hour and 60 minutes

B. **Listen and repeat these words.**

I	hide	behind	drive	arrive	light
bicycle	right	decide	hike	fly	knife

Listen and repeat these sentences.

1. Hide behind the bike.

2. Let's hike on a nice island.

3. I don't arrive tired.

4. Mike's a wild child.

C. **In words that follow the pattern consonant *i* consonant *e*, the *i* is usually pronounced like the *i* in *bike*. Listen to the following words. Circle the words that follow this rule.**

drive	arrive	expensive	time
police	knife	live	hide

The *i* in words that end in *–ild* and *–ight* are also pronounced this way. What other words do you know that follow this rule?

D. **Sentences have stress patterns just like words. In most sentences, content words like *Mary*, *apple*, and *happy* are stressed, and function words like *he*, *to*, *was*, and *but* are reduced. Listen to this children's poem and underline the words that are stressed.**

> Mary had a little lamb,
> Its fleece* was white as snow,
> And everywhere that Mary went,
> The lamb was sure to go.
>
> *Fleece is a lamb's fur (hair).*

Now listen again and repeat the poem.

E. Dictation. You will hear a dictation three times. The first time, listen only. The second time, write. The third time, check your work. When you hear the word *period*, write "." at the end of the sentence.

_____

_____

_____

_____

_____

_____

_____

_____

F. Listen to this commercial from a tour company, and fill in the information in the form below.

Name _____

Offers tours to _____

_____

_____

Advantages of tours _____

_____

_____

_____

Prices of Tours _____ to _____

Telephone number _____

G. Think of a vacation spot in your country and write a radio advertisement for it. Read your advertisement to your partner.

unit 24

I Can't Wait to Get Wet!

In this unit you will practice: /ɛ/ /eʸ/ (*wet/wait*)

Pronunciation Tool
See page 99.

Before you begin: Discuss the following questions with your classmates.

◆ Are there rules in public parks and beaches in your country?

◆ What are they?

A. **Read the questions. Then listen to the conversation and answer them.**

1. Where are the speakers?
   a. at the beach
   b. at the swimming pool
   c. in a park

2. The beach is very
   a. crowded.
   b. large.
   c. quiet.

3. Which things can't you do there?
   a. swim
   b. have a picnic
   c. fish
   d. play radios

B. **Listen to these pairs of words.**

1. wet   wait   3. tell   tale   5. met   mate

2. less lace   4. red   raid

Now listen again and repeat the words.

Listen to the vowels in these words. Put a check (√) under the word below that has the same vowel sound.

	wet	wait
1. gave	____	____
2. red	____	____
3. step	____	____
4. play	____	____
5. belt	____	____

Listen to these sentences and write the missing words.

1. A _____ is a story.

2. You gave me _____.

3. Some women like to wear _____.

4. Can you _____ this for me?

5. This paper is _____.

C. **In words that follow the pattern consonant _e_ consonant, the _e_ is usually pronounced like the _e_ in _wet_. Listen to the following words. Circle the syllables that follow this rule.**

send   new/er   men   ne/ver   cen/tur/y

bal/let   te/le/phone   tired   help   jewel/ry

There are three common ways to spell the vowel sound in _late_.

__a__e as in _cake_

__a i __ as in _raid_*

__ __a y as in _play_

*One common exception is the word_ said.

Rhyming race. Think of as many words as you can that rhyme with the words at the top of each column. They do not have to have the same spelling.

cake	raid	play
_____	_____	_____
_____	_____	_____
_____	_____	_____
_____	_____	_____

D. **Dictation.** You will hear a dictation three times. The first time, listen only. The second time, write. The third time, check your work.

_____

_____

_____

_____

_____

_____

_____

_____

E. **Read the following signs. Then listen to the conversation and put a check (√) next to the signs that appear in the park.**

F. **Think of some places in your country where there are special rules about what you can and can't do. Tell your partner.**

First You Open the Hood...

Pronunciation Tool
See page 99.

In this unit you will practice: /ʊ/ /uʷ/ (*pull/pool*)

Before you begin: Discuss the following questions with your classmates.

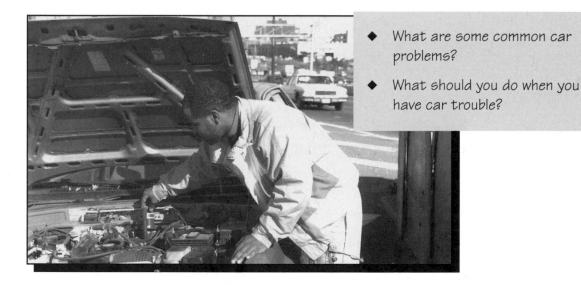

◆ What are some common car problems?

◆ What should you do when you have car trouble?

A. **Read the questions. Then listen to the conversation and answer them.**

1. Who is speaking?
   a. Luke and his father
   b. Luke and his brother
   c. Luke and his friend

2. What time of day is it?
   a. morning
   b. afternoon
   c. night

3. Which things should Luke do?
   a. Put up the hood of the car.
   b. Turn on the headlights.
   c. Tie a white cloth on the antenna.
   d. Lock the doors.
   e. Listen to the radio.
   f. Turn on the flashers.

B. Listen to these pairs of words.

1. pull   pool
2. could   cooed
3. full   fool
4. should   shooed
5. stood   stewed

Now listen again and repeat the words.

Listen to these sentences and fill in the missing words.

1. There's _____ _____ at the _____.

2. _____ _____ _____ your _____ in the

   _____?

3. He likes _____, and he's a _____ _____.

4. _____ _____ buy a _____ _____

   _____ _____?

5. The woman _____ not _____ _____ for

   _____ !

Now listen again and repeat the sentences.

Look at the words you wrote in the sentences above. Which words have the same vowel sound as the word *pull*? Which ones have the same vowel sound as the word *pool*? Write the words in the correct column below. Make sure you have spelled the words correctly.

pull	*pool*

C.

Listen and write the words *would, wouldn't, should, shouldn't, could,* or *couldn't* in the blanks. Note that the *l* in these words is silent.

1. _____ you get her a cup of coffee?

2. You _____ leave so early.

3. We _____ see the bridge from our house.

4. What _____ you like to drink?

5. I _____ like anything, thank you.

D.

Listen to the directions on how to do these exercises. Then choose the correct group of pictures: 1, 2, or 3.

First Exercise

Second Exercise

E.

Think of an exercise you know. Make some notes about how to do the exercise. Ask your teacher if you need help. Explain to your partner how to do the exercise.

It's 61° and Cloudy.

In this unit you will practice: /æ/ /ɑ/ (*map/mop*)

Pronunciation Tool
See page 99.

Before you begin: Discuss the following questions with your classmates.

- ◆ What's the weather like in this picture?

- ◆ What's your favorite kind of weather? Why?

A. **Read the questions. Then listen to the weather report and answer them.**

1. What's the weather like right now?
   a. rainy
   b. sunny
   c. cloudy

2. What's the weather going to be like later?
   a. rainy
   b. sunny
   c. cloudy

3. What will the high temperature be today?
   a. 61°
   b. 68°
   c. 88°

4. How's the weather going to be tomorrow?
   a. rainy
   b. sunny
   c. cloudy

B. **Listen and repeat these pairs of words.**

1. map   mop
2. can   con
3. band   bond
4. rack   rock
5. an   on
6. cab   cob

Listen and write the words you hear. Then check (√) the column under the word that has the same vowel sound.

		map	*mop*
1.	_____	_____	_____
2.	_____	_____	_____
3.	_____	_____	_____
4.	_____	_____	_____
5.	_____	_____	_____

Now listen again and repeat the words.

Listen to these sentences and fill in the missing words.

1. Give _____ a _____ of _____.

2. He _____ to _____ and get a _____ in the _____.

3. Put the _____ in my _____.

4. Wear your _____; the sun's _____.

C. **Listen to these sentences and fill in the blanks with *can* or *can't*.**

1. She _____ go in the water.

2. You _____ play tennis tomorrow.

3. _____ we leave now?

4. Who _____ speak Spanish?

Now listen again and repeat the sentences.

D. **Listen and repeat these sentences. Be careful to stress only the content words.**

1. Please give me the rock in the can.

2. Oh dear! I left my new mop in the cab!

3. The band plays dance music at a disco.

4. Dan had a good job, but he lost it.

5. Pam has a great collection of early rock music.

E. Listen to the weather report. Draw the weather symbols on the map for each city. Then listen again and write the high and low temperatures for each city next to that city.

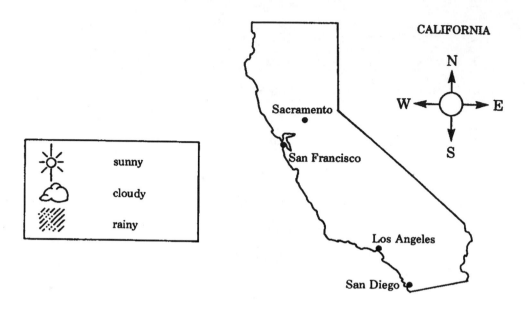

CALIFORNIA

sunny

cloudy

rainy

F. Look at this map of New York. Decide on the weather for each city. Then tell your partner.

NEW YORK

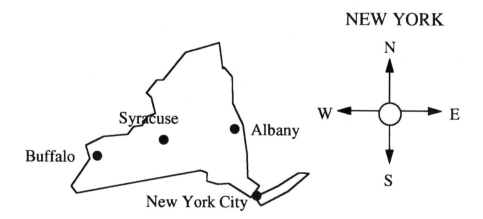

unit *27*

I Got a Robe and Socks.

Pronunciation Tool
See page 99.

In this unit you will practice: /ɑ/ /oʷ/ (*want/won't*)

Before you begin: Discuss the following questions with your classmates.

◆ If you buy something and it's not right, what do you do?

◆ What do you think this man is saying to himself?

A. **Read the questions. Then listen to the conversation and answer them.**

1. How does Mr. Thompson feel?

_____

2. What mistake did the store make?

_____

3. What is the store going to do?

_____

B. Listen and repeat these pairs of words.

1. want   won't   4. sock   soak
2. clock   cloak   5. not   note
3. rob   robe   6. got   goat

Listen to these sentences and write the missing words in the blanks.

1. Please _____ _____ in the _____

    _____.

2. I _____ to the _____ in the museum of _____

    _____.

3. She _____ put her _____ in the _____

    _____.

Look at the words you wrote in the sentences above. Which words have the same vowel sound as the word *got*? Which ones have the same vowel sound as the word *goat*? Write the words in the correct column below. Make sure you spell the words correctly.

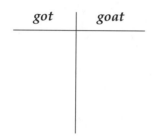

got | *goat*

Now listen again and repeat the sentences.

C. There are several ways to spell the vowel sound /oʷ/. Look at the words above. Find an example for each spelling.

1. _____ oa _____
2. _____ o _____ _____
3. _____ _____ow
4. _____ _____ o _____ e

The words below are all spelled consonant *o* consonant *e*. Circle the ones that do not have the vowel sound /oʷ/.

drove   some   wrote   love   come   spoke   before

Listen to these sentences and fill in the missing words.

1. _____ _____ you tomorrow.

2. She _____ _____ without him.

3. We _____ _____ go soon.

4. _____ _____ _____ answer my question?

5. _____ _____ _____ arrive?

E. **Listen to the conversation. Write down the quantity, the color, and the size of (1) the things Alex received and (2) the things Alex ordered.**

1. Received

	Quigley's Department Store San Francisco, California		
ITEM	*quantity*	*color*	*size*
raincoat	_____	_____	_____
shirt	_____	_____	_____
pants	_____	_____	_____

2. Ordered

	Quigley's Department Store San Francisco, California		
ITEM	*quantity*	*color*	*size*
raincoat	_____	_____	_____
shirt	_____	_____	_____
pants	_____	_____	_____

F. **Complete the order form. Then call your partner and place an order.**

ITEM	quantity	size	color
pants			
shirt			
coat			

unit 28

Could You Take a Memo, Please?

In this unit you will practice: /ʊ/ /ʌ/ (look/luck)

Pronunciation Tool
See page 99.

Before you begin: Discuss the following question with your classmates.

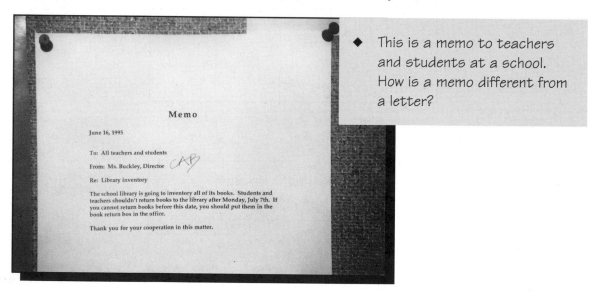

Memo

June 16, 1995

To: All teachers and students

From: Ms. Buckley, Director

Re: Library inventory

The school library is going to inventory all of its books. Students and teachers shouldn't return books to the library after Monday, July 7th. If you cannot return books before this date, you should put them in the book return box in the office.

Thank you for your cooperation in this matter.

◆ This is a memo to teachers and students at a school. How is a memo different from a letter?

A. Read these questions. Then listen to the conversation and answer them.

1. Who is this conversation between?

_____

2. Listen to the memo and compare it with the one above. How are they different?

_____

B. Listen and repeat these pairs of words.

1. look   luck
2. could   cud
3. put   putt
4. book   buck
5. stood   stud

Listen to these sentences. Write *1* under the words that contain the same vowel sound as *look* and *2* under the words that contain the same vowel sound as *luck*.

1. Mother doesn't have enough.
2. The woman could die in the flood.
3. The hood of the car was full of soot.
4. The customer put the wool on the chair.
5. They tried to pull the bull with the truck.

C. There are several ways to spell the vowel sound in *look*. Look at the sentences above. Find an example for each spelling.

__ *oo* __

__ *u* __

__ *ould*

There are several ways to spell the vowel sound in *luck*. Find an example for each spelling in the sentences above.

__ __ u __ __

__ __ oo __

__ __ ough

D. Listen and repeat these sentences. Be careful to stress only the content words.

1. The children are looking at the toys.

2. Pearl S. Buck was a writer in the 1940s and 1950s.

3. Should we go on Tuesday or Wednesday?

4. The class studies pronunciation.

5. Everyone likes my mother's spaghetti.

E. Listen to the conversation. Then write the memo.

```
MEMO

DATE:

TO:

FROM:  Elaine Rogers, Office Manager

SUBJECT:


          Everyone who plans to
```

F. Write a memo to your employees. Then dictate it to your partner.

unit 29

How Do I Get to the Public Library?

In this unit you will practice: /ʌ/ /ɔ/ (done/dawn)

| Pronunciation Tool |
| See page 99. |

Before you begin: Discuss the following question with your classmates.

◆ What do you think this man is asking the police officer?

A. **Read these questions. Then listen to the conversation and answer them.**

1. Who is Dave talking to?

   _____

2. Where does Dave want to go?

   _____

3. Which ways should Dave turn?

   _____

4. Which two places are on Dawn Drive?

   _____

B. **Listen and repeat these pairs of words.**

1. done   dawn
2. but   bought
3. fun   fawn
4. pun   pawn
5. flood   flawed
6. cud   caught
7. hull   hall

Listen to these sentences. Underline the syllables that have the same vowel sound as *dawn*.

1. Will the audience applaud?
2. He often plays with his dog on the lawn.
3. There's a bookcase along the wall in the hall.

Now listen again and repeat the sentences.

C. **There are several ways to spell the vowel sound in *dawn*. Look at the sentences above. Find an example for each spelling.**

1. __ __ __ __ au __
2. __ o __
3. __ aw __
4. __ all

D. Dictation. You will hear a dictation three times. The first time, listen only. The second time, write. The third time, check your work.

_____

_____

_____

_____

_____

_____

E. Listen to the conversation and draw arrows to show the way to the supermarket.

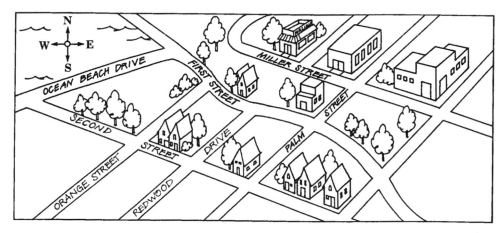

F. Tell your partner how to get from school to one of these places:

       your house

       a bookstore

       a supermarket

unit 30

Review

A. Read the questions. Then listen to the conversation and answer them.

1. The speakers are talking
   a. on the telephone.
   b. in an office.
   c. in Alex's house.

2. Alex wants to make _____ reservations.
   a. train
   b. boat
   c. plane

3. Alex will stay in Hawaii for _____ days.
   a. ten
   b. twenty
   c. thirty

4. Alex is going to Hawaii
   a. with a friend.
   b. alone.
   c. with two other people.

Listen again and check (√) the sentences you hear.

1. a. How may I help you today, Mr. Stern?
   b. Can I help you today, Mr. Stern?
   c. How can I help you today, Mr. Stern?

2. a. I want first class tickets.
   b. I'd like first class tickets.
   c. I like first class tickets.

3. a. I'll call you back after I make the reservations.
   b. I can call you back after I make the reservations.
   c. Call me back after you make the reservations.

B. **Listen to these sentences and circle the word you hear.**

1. That hill's/heel's too high.

2. I'll carry the cot/coat.

3. That's a very good bond/band.

4. That's my map/mop.

5. He's going to leave/live alone.

6. She says she has a pen/pain.

7. That cloak/clock was a gift from Dan.

Now listen again and repeat the sentences.

Listen to these sentences and write the words in the order you hear them.

1. (fun, fawn) _____ _____

2. (pull, pool) _____ _____

3. (wet, wait) _____ _____

4. (want, won't) _____ _____

5. (rich, reach) _____ _____

Now listen again and repeat the sentences.

C. **Read this conversation. Underline the stressed words.**

BETSY: Guess what, Jim! We can go by car tonight!
JIM: That's nice. Did you get your car fixed?
BETSY: No, I didn't get it fixed. I got a new one!
JIM: Wow! We've got a new car!
BETSY: We?
JIM: Sorry. I mean you've got a new car.

Now listen to the conversation. Did you underline the correct words? Then practice the conversation with a classmate.

D. **Listen to these sentences and write *will*, *'ll*, or *won't* in the blanks.**

1. You _____ see him soon.

2. When _____ they watch television?

3. _____ you stay a while longer?

4. We _____ go if they do.

5. If he stays, he _____ see the game.

E. **Listen to the conversation and fill in the travel agency form.**

LEISURE TIME TRAVEL AGENCY

NAME/S _____

_____

_____

AIRLINE _____ FLIGHT NUMBER _____

DEPARTS _____ AT _____

ARRIVES _____ AT _____

_____ CLASS

SEAT #'S _____ _____ _____

TOTAL PRICE $ _____

Appendix

Pronunciation Tools

A. Mouth Maps. These diagrams show tongue and lip positions. Sounds which have the same tongue and lip positions differ in other ways such as manner of articulation, voicing, and aspiration. The presence or absence of voicing is indicated in voiced/voiceless pairs.

1. **/l/ /n/ /t/** (voiceless)
   /d/ (voiced)
   Examples: lip, pill, not, can, tin, sent, do, did

2. **/r/**
   Examples: run, tar

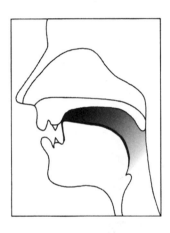

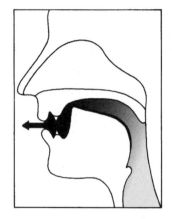

3. **/k/** (voiceless)
   /g/ (voiced)
   Examples: king, crack, go, bag

4. **/f/** (voiceless)
   /v/ (voiced)
   Examples: fun, knife, van, cave

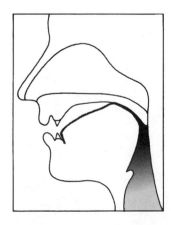

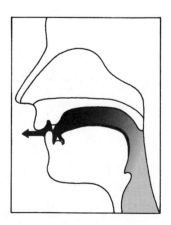

5. /θ/ (voiceless)
/ð/ (voiced)
Examples: **th**in, smoo**th**,
the, soo**the**

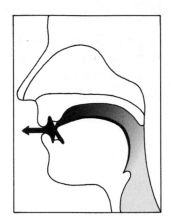

6. /s/ (voiceless)
/z/ (voiced)
Examples: **S**ue, bo**ss**, **z**oo, knee**s**

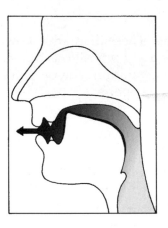

7. /tʃ/ (voiceless)
/dʒ/ (voiced)
Examples: **ch**in, mat**ch**,
jam, ba**dge**

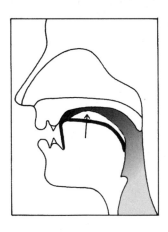

8. /y/
Examples: **y**es, milli**o**n

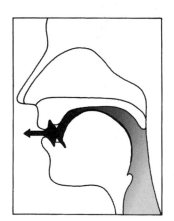

9. /h/
Examples: have, perhaps

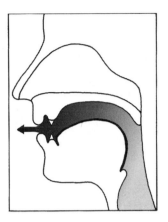

B. Vowel Chart

The Vowel Chart

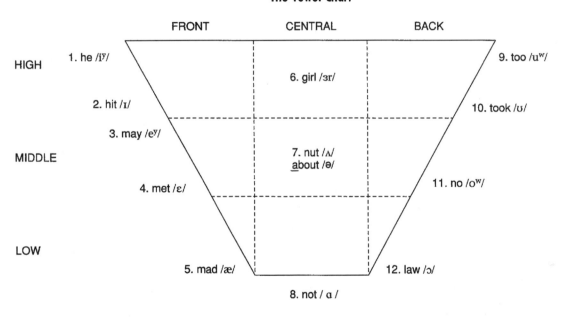

FRONT   CENTRAL   BACK

HIGH   1. he /iʸ/   6. girl /ɜr/   9. too /uʷ/

2. hit /ɪ/   10. took /ʊ/

3. may /eʸ/

MIDDLE   7. nut /ʌ/
<u>a</u>bout /ə/

4. met /ɛ/   11. no /oʷ/

LOW

5. mad /æ/   12. law /ɔ/

8. not / ɑ /